Over the Edge

poems

Norbert Hirschhorn

Holland Park Press London

Published by Holland Park Press 2023
Copyright © Norbert Hirschhorn 2023

First Edition

British Library Cataloguing-in-Publication Data
A catalogue record for this book is available from the British Library

ISBN 978-1-907320-99-6

Cover designed by Reactive Graphics

Printed and bound by
CPI Group (UK) Ltd, Croydon CR0 4YY

www.hollandparkpress.co.uk

For Cynthia

CONTENTS

A House in the Woods

853 Riverside Drive
(New York City)

Brothers in Exile

In the Beginning

A House in the Woods

Death in the Air

Up to 1,500 birds on the Atlantic Flyway smashed
into skyscrapers overnight. The slaughter shook bird
watchers. (Philadelphia Inquirer, October 7, 2020)

> Dear friends, not just birders, all of us.
> Something disrupted the birds' inerrant flight.
> Electronic noise, perhaps, from people tweeting,
> texting, zooming during lock down.
> Let us then say their names, as we do all who die of
> war, virus, injustice:

Goldfinchoriolechickadeegrosbeakjayjuncofinch
cardinalflickersiskinnuthatchhummingbirdbluebird
warblerredpollblackbird

For Michael Longley

A Burnt Offering

Boiled eggs, dark bread, pale ale
and a friend. One candle, a sudden breeze.

The world a trap, a taunt. In its sweetness,
a betrayal. A squirrel spirals the young oak, evading
the gyrating hawk.

Consciousness crossing a river in spate
on algae-coated rocks. Crack of an ankle.

Moon keeps tugging away from earth, yet held
in thrall. Before you, dear Huntress, I stand like a mooncalf.

Mass grave, earth stirred for three days.
Those who endured, they understand –

Heaven but a palm's breadth above the ground,
why we rise off our heels saying, *holy holy holy.*

A holly blue butterfly lands on my arm.

AGAINST SOLITUDE

1.
The Mississippi River St. Anthony Falls an incessant roar
I can feel from my fifth-floor window & I see life –
Our bald eagle pair winging back from fishing, flocks of
geese puncturing the sky on their way north.

Bounded by sun risen to my left (glisters from
windows across), setting to my right (torching
buildings in the east). Bridges with traffic, walkers
bike riders, joggers. I'm not at all lonely. Out there
is in here. A lucky life.

Norbert, what crap. Days since the city began
to burn. Helicopters bombinate the sky,
people enraged, filling the streets.

2.
two thirty am   wind-still   cloudless
full moon (dream catcher) hangs above
an office building   white   cold

no birds flying   no cars on the
bridge   no sirens   no insomniac
walker with a dog   no one coming

home drunk   only my obsessions
to remind me I'm still here   but there's
no 'here'   only (maybe) end-of-days

3.
Solitude. I wish there were such,
the world too much with us.
Hissing tinnitus without reprieve
I'd have to pretend to compose a hymn –

To Solitude

except I meditate in the dark,
brood on my failings in the dark.
Not a hymn but a hum.

REPORT FROM INSIDE A SNOW GLOBE

We farm potatoes. We are at peace.
Our town's poor but decent, our pleasure's

sitting still on park benches watching
pigeons perch on the General's head.

The lucent vault that serves as sky
turns from day-bright to amber to indigo.

True, we suffer earthquakes we call
The Great Shakings, heralded by

a shadow encroaching overhead.
Wind and whistling scatter ash and ember

on the pond, schoolyard, the burial ground.
But nothing important, thank God, ever falls down.

Soon, stillness again; and we try not to remember.

EARTH'S HUM

*(Earth's 'hum' – a product of storm energy over the oceans,
below the threshold of human hearing. BBC News)*

Why is she humming
and to whom? About?
Days, nights, going and coming
(while her children cavort),

spinning, tilting to one side,
around a restless sun –
indifferent to anything we may say or find,
someday to flare, flame, be done.

What melody does she thrum?
A subliminal lay of the sublime,
in minor key some *Liebestraum*?
'We have time, my darling, we only have time.'

A lullaby? Cradlesong only newborns discern,
but forgotten in life's turmoil and noise,
roughshod-ridden to make them unlearn
all ethereal joys.

Or, while tending olive trees, anemones,
some private rum-tiddly-tum:
after four billion years, finally at ease
from cosmic perturbations, *Sturm und Drang*.

Whatever –
    in a million years or sooner
human ruckus will be done
and earth's air heard but by moon or
stars, or newer life-forms yet to come.

Until the End of Time
(For Brian Greene)

Death I understand: my flesh rejoins the universe
like sea water escaping a cracked amphora.
The way, they say, I inhale molecules breathed out
by Jesus. Another kind of resurrection.

But how did I get here in the first place?

A little wanderer, in what green room was I waiting
to come on stage? In what bardo antechamber
awaiting summons, like a quantum particle kept in
suspense (there) (not there)? Or, washing ashore
from fathomless depths, laughing and crying with
my first breath.

And where did these luscious figs come from?

AFFLICTIONS

I'm only the stories I make up about myself: homesick
for places I've never been, nostalgic for moments yet to
begin, remembering what will never happen.
The life I lead is not my own.

> memories shimmer
> fire damp across a dark lake
> veined wings harmonic

My way home grows longer each day. Beware the
Chronophage – Loved ones, strangers, email bots who
cannibalize your minutes, days, years by bits and nibbles.
To eat another being is disgusting, but the necessary of
the world. We're all consumed.

The Talmud tells of the ram having but one voice when
alive, yet seven after he dies: Horns to make two shofars,
hip bones two pipes, skin a drum, gut strings for
lyre and harp.

> All bodies are a kind of music.

The worst evil people can do is making it impossible
to believe in a loving God, abandoned to the vastness.
God is the father who lost his children.
Comfort ye.

The world burns. Church spires crumble, bring down the
sky. Forest berries shrivel. We are perpetually in grief.
If not, should be.

    brown pall over all
    the city   diesel exhaust
    whistling in the ears

But I am responsible,
for as the Talmud teaches:

> *The world was created for me,*
> *the world exists because of me.*

SAILING WITH THE PLEIADES

Even as I jog the streets of New Haven,
speeds up to three one-thousandths
a kilometer a second, saying hi there!

to Annette – sidewalk flower seller –
to trash gleaners, a cop, and caretaker Bill
of the Grove Street Cemetery,

Earth twirls me on its hip, east to west,
gyrating through seasons, while Sun pilots
its argosy of planets and asteroids

around Milky Way's center – two hundred
fifty million years to make one circuit –
and our dear little galaxy sails on:

silent, ghostly, accelerating in free fall
toward the *Terrible Crystal*:   God.
God? Who created Himself from Nothing?

He's flying away from us, faster than light.
Ahhh, let him go, trouble from the start,
or where was he when we needed him most?

And another thing: the way a tsunami in Hokkaido
cancels a wave off Cape Cod, consider
that I'm alone this night, running the lanes

of the graveyard, abandoned
at the speed of thought,
eyes shut tight, hardly moving at all.

My Many Moons

Once over a mosque in Damascus –
once over the sea off Beirut – crescent moon
and morning star against a heart-stop sky.

Guide and guardian over desert tracks –
and when born from a predawn thunderstorm,
that rarest sight: a spectral lunar rainbow.

A sickle engraved on a twilight cloth –
al-hilal – announces a new month,
my latest of many.

When eclipsed by earth, *blood moon.*
When solitary in winter: *white stone.*
Nimbus-crowned: heralding spring rain.

From behind a scrim of cloud
beams filter through a tangle of cypress
whose roots twist about men's bones.

My many moons. Were they enough?
My epitaph, *Not Enough.*

Anatomy Lesson: The Philtrum

An old country tale my mother told:
an angel kissed my upper lip to make me
forget my Edenic life before this life –
sweet eternities forced to forsake,
traded in for nights of lust, days of hard-labor.

I was one of the luckier ones.
                                    Others,
bruised by *afreet*, antiseptically labeled
FAS, *fetal alcohol syndrome*,
recall only chaos, rage, the broken cord.

Or, that needy girl with a cleft-stricken face
mocked as hare-lip – beauty askew,
ready to kiss any who'd care to have her.

O dear angel: spare us, kiss us to redemption,
drown us in your hollows.

A Story About Divorce

it's like

some roach crawled out from the woodwork:
with a book, a shoe, I crush it,
grab the carcass with layers of tissue,

and tremble, as I flush and flush and flush.
never such hatred when squeezing a pimple
or gutting a fish.

and yet,

what if I festered for years in a scurfy cell,
one tiny barred hole ten feet above my head
to let in gray light?

would it emerge from the drainpipe
trailing essence of sweet wormwood
on its cunning little feet?

would I lie there bemused like a Gulliver?
watch it skitter across my hands? feel it savor
my lips with its waving antennae,

sneak inside my nostril to flatten
against moist membranes
like a blind man in a cave –

until I sneezed

and saw it somersault against the wall?
would we both laugh,
then apologize,

    begin the game again?

Virginia Creeper

Five-fingered ivy, born in a neighbor's yard,
climbs a brick wall, mounts the side
of the terrace house next door. Along its stem
tendrils emerge to penetrate tiny
fissures, clinching like a cragsman.

Alluring invader – so green in summer,
blood-red in fall – crawls on to our balcony,
aims for downspouts and roof tiles. At night,
beneath Orion, a solitary bine
pokes through our transom window. Soon,
we'll lie entwined as in a *Briar Wood*.

A DISQUISITION ON TIME
(With help from Stephen Hawking)

Time is only what a clock reads: my wristwatch,
grandfather's pendulum, the steady oscillation
of a cesium molecule,

       tick   tock   tick

Time keeps two bodies from occupying the exact
same space at once – but when I'm inside you,
my dearest, we interrogate the thesis.

       tick   tock   tick

Time's arrow flies forward as entropy rises.
My decay is what I measure as *Time* –
just one lonely moment after another.

       tock

SPELLBOUND

At each beginning of each new beginning –
school, job, retreat by the sea – he fell in love.
Always the same person: solemn, thin,
no makeup, a way of brushing back a strand
that made him nearly cry with longing.

They'd walk along a corniche holding hands –
or through woods, or through galleries –
something about her hand he knew
even in the dark.

Then – Gone. Gone.

He looked for her.
Perhaps he saw her,
or thought he saw her,
threading the crowd off Piccadilly,
across a square in Siena.
He'd wave, or maybe
tried to wave, call out her name
but her name choked in his throat.

Much later, he woke to find her
standing at the foot of his bed.

> *Who are you?* he whispered.
> *How did I ever come to know you?*

THE CALL

4:33 by the bedside alarm,
jangled from a dream,
blankets tangled – has someone died?

A muted voice, echoing,
one he'd heard before.

I know why you're calling. Who are you?
Irrelevant.
I've tried to be good.
You only think you're good.
Everyone deserves to be held.
Don't presume.

The moon hung over the high-rise opposite,
frozen like a tombstone.

I'm generous, all my friends will tell you.
You never bought Big Issue from that homeless person.

Stop. Stop. I hate this.
I'm sure you do.
Who are you? Is this a nightmare?

Jagged clouds eroded Orion.

I am who I am
Maybe an angel I'm supposed to wrestle?
Throw out my hip, become a cripple?
You're already crippled.

Wait! You're my muse, right? Bringing me a poem?
Nothing so pitiful as a would-be poet.
You make me feel like a worm impaled on a hook
of indifference.
That's pathetic.

A sharp wind blew up, tree limbs beckoned.

Please, give me some ease.
Not to be had.

Then let me ask you something.
Go ahead.

Why does it take me so long to leave the house?
You know, forget this, forget that, recheck the stove,
go back for the umbrella...

You're afraid you'll die.
I am afraid.
Good then. Let's go.

FOR MEN WHO LIE AWAKE AT NIGHT
(In the night/ each foot has nothing to love/
but the other foot. Ruth Stone, 'Sorrow')

He remembers each least mistake,
so long ago still feels like yesterday.

All his life just rehearsal, a play opening and closing
the same night.

An unnecessary person, a tesseral misfit.

He dreams bestial: piss, shit, fuck, bleed, rot.
Checks the sheets each time he gets up to pee.

Lying awake at night, *Nachas* has a twin named *Tsuris*.

Calendar makers have walked off the job.
A blind man taps his cane on the cobbles.

Lying awake at night I lay me down bless us O Lord
and these thy

What to do with this half-mast erection?
Even in paradise mosquitos poke holes
in the screen.

Like the fly in a vat of broth who surrenders:
I've drunk, eaten, bathed. I'm ready.

Nachas – delight; especially pride in one's children
Tsuris – sorrow, woe, troubles

A Train Engineer's Last Interview

Oh sure. I loved the night shifts. California Zephyr
from Denver to Omaha. All by myself.

See, with diesel you no longer needed a second
man in the cab, which was fine by me.

Well, you get a chatterbox they want to tell you
their whole life story. Last guy kept a flask in his
hip pocket. Driving alone suited me.

Something about those long, straight tracks.
Sometimes a full moon lighting the way,
crows lifting off as we approached a giant oak.
You had to look out for deer though.

Yes, one time a moose so large he could have
derailed us, but smart enough to give way when I
blasted the horn, his nostrils blowing steam.

What happened to a buddy of mine was – a drunk
driver fast asleep on the crossing. It takes a mile
to stop when traveling at full throttle.

Eight hours and some, short-haul. I'd grab sleep on
the station master's cot, then return by day. After
supper and a couple hours with the wife and kids,
good to go again.

> *May life be as precise*
> *as a railroad pocket watch*
> *and borne without crossings*

A HOUSE IN THE WOODS

House without doors or windows.
Neither cellar nor attic. No front steps.
Inside,

a single room, unlit. No pictures,
no mirrors – impossible to see yourself here.
Alone. Your voice an echo off

the alabaster wall, reverberating
until you stop calling *hello   hello*?
You finger your way along the plaster, and realise:

no corners, a circular room, wall blending
in with floor on which you tread noiselessly,
reading the wall like Braille from a blank page.

You step away from wall, become lost – unable
to find your way back – trawling in circles.
Sit. Wait. Lie down. Fall asleep.

You do know what this is about, don't you?

DARK-TIME WINTER BLUES

1.
in frigid Minnesota
thirty below
an old farmer got lost
in a whiteout of snow
body found frozen   yes
to his own backhoe

stumbling in the dark
on an iced-over pond
unsure of footing
on an icy pond
too anxious to get home   yes
crack   almost drowned

2.
each November we
pull up geraniums   yes
hang 'em by their roots
in the cellar half alive
hung by their roots   I say
still   they revive

replant me so
when you move on my love
when you gotta go
no longer in love
still my love will survive
my love   yes   I'll survive

FINLANDIA WOOD

Storm-lashed lakes grow still,
blue pools reflecting pine, spruce, larch –
preening their platonic selves.

Skinny birches race their siblings
to reach the cornflower sky – in time
they'll slow, thicken, become good citizens.

Their ciliate tips wave outside my window,
incised against the sky like intaglio.
Bohemian waxwings rise in flocks, taken fright.

River Vantaa – dark avatar – marches
downstream, a force unseen, bobbing
brown crests, kneading brown troughs.

(A young aspen collapses into the water.)

Here in north latitudes thunder rumbles
in higher timbre, viola not cello,
wakens dreamers.

A lone box elder on a Northern farm
stands vigil under full moonlight, casting
scant shadow on the frosted stubble.

Barn, an abandoned plow, a log-framed
two-room house where a farmer
sleeps outstretched (or perhaps

there's no one there aware
of the moon overhead),
his right cheek laid hard on his hand.

THE BLESSÉD MOTHER

They used the woman as slavey: COME HERE!
CARRY THIS! BRING THAT! SHOUTING, because she spoke
little English. She heard horses snuffling in their stalls,
Spitfires overhead. At noon, her lunch half-hour, she
heard church bells. 'The Angelus,' said the Irish maids.
'Turn your thoughts to God and the Blesséd Mother.'
In the garden, she sat under the laburnum tree, its
golden chains reminding her of lindens in Vienna whose
perfume infiltrated that last summer before their escape.
Her toddler son was made to be still. He was still;
and years after, still. A sepia photograph shows his lips
trembling. She dries sweet red peppers for paprika to add
to the goulash.

*853 Riverside Drive
(New York City)*

MIGRANTS TO 853 RIVERSIDE DRIVE

We left Liverpool, England, November 1944,
on a cargo ship, *The Manchester Shipper*, going to
America, traveling zig zag for eighteen days in a convoy
because German U-boats were still out there prowling.
I remember target practice from our small forward guns,
bang bang bang. When we reached New York Harbor,
I became aware of seagulls. Seagulls, circling the Statue
of Liberty, screeching. What are they? I asked my
mother. *Möwen*, she replied, *Möwen*.

I grew up in New York City, a six-story apartment
building with a flat roof where clotheslines were strung
and where I helped mother put up sheets and towels just
come out of washing. I would edge over to the waist-high
parapet, and imagine myself flying to the next building
over. It was my first sense of suicide, which mother tried
not long after, sticking her head in a gas oven.

My father couldn't carry a tune if his life depended
on it, which at one time it did when the SS made him
gargle *Hatikvah*, the Jewish national anthem.

Look, We Made It to America

A three-room apartment,
rent-controlled (we couldn't afford otherwise).
Look,
once upscale: uniformed doorman, concierge.
Look,
my father said sadly, it isn't like that five-room,
elegant flat in Vienna we had to flee.

Look,
now giant cockroaches emerge
from the basement whose dank interior
I explored, watching out for the growly
superintendent, Old George,
who prowled his troll-kingdom basement.

My Mother at 853 Riverside Drive

As I rounded the corner
coming home from play
I could see our fourth floor
kitchen window, dim lightbulb
backlighting her shadow.

She always looked out for me,
thinking I wasn't safe until
she saw me, knew I hadn't
been run over, wasn't beaten
by anti-Semite teens
who lay in waiting. Because

that was how she grew up.
Oh c'mon Ma, this is America.

She Who Never Made It to 853 Riverside Drive

What should I call the baby who died
before I was born?   Sister.

If Gertrude hadn't given up her life –
(ill before penicillin) –
would I have existed at all?

My mother grieved unbearably. So much so
she never raised a stone over Gertie's grave.

Abandoned her to holy soil in the Jewish section,
children's portion, in the *Zentralfriedhof.*
Perhaps, on the way, the good *Bürgers* of Vienna

bellowed out, *Schmutzige Jüdin.*

Nine months before my conception,
another nine months to my birth –

eighteen months: in Hebrew numerology,
khai, khet-yod, which also means 'life'.
Why Jews give charity in multiples of *khai*.

The Kabbalah says
the world was created from letters,
khet yod (*khai*) an emanation of God closest to us.

I became the replacement child,
bound up in the bond of life.

My Mother Tries on a New Floral Housecoat at 853 Riverside Drive

Sitting at my 8th grade homework in the alcove by
the kitchen I smelled something strange. I turned

to see my mother sitting calmly, wearing her new
housecoat, her chair facing the gas-oven door.

'Ma! What are you doing? You're scaring me.'
She looked up.

'No, darling, I didn't mean to frighten you, please don't
worry,
      but don't tell your father.'

ME, AT 853 RIVERSIDE DRIVE

My feet drag through the overgrown grass
trying to go home.
But home, what is it?
Home recedes with each step I take,

walking away from me!
Only the road knows the way to go.
My fault, to believe I could just leave. Now,
when I need it, home won't let me come back.

CALLING HOME TO 853 RIVERSIDE DRIVE

I tried calling mother from a public phone, but
clumsily mis-fingered the buttons, had to start over
and over and over. The robotic voice asked for a
credit card (using your dial pad) and password.
People behind me angry, but I finally got through:
'Hi Mom, it's Norbert, I'm coming home.'
Norbert, who's he? and hung up.

Over the Edge at 853 Riverside Drive

He gave mother his weekly pay packet, and she
returned his allowance for cigarettes, NY Post,
Daily News, gas for the Plymouth, shoeshine
on Fridays.

She had to manage on little, and did, saying,
for instance, 'Willi, on your way home, please pick up...'
He went along with her game because she was a good
manager.

We lacked for little. Until he got fired.

Then, I had to work after school, sweeping floors:
hair from the barber's, blood from the butcher's,
keeping some coins as my allowance, stored safely
in a ceramic piggy bank. Safely.

Until one day I found it hammer-smashed, money gone.
I shouted at my father, 'You stole my money!'
That's when he lost it, letting out a roar like a bull
slaughtered. Roar, more brutal in German: *Brüllen*.

Ach, er ist so blöd, my mother mocked.

Until just now, as I recover this memory,
I'd always thought his rage was about my insolence.
No. It wasn't. Something else. Over the edge.

My Father Escapes 853 Riverside Drive

On one exquisite spring day,
my father gave it up.
Walked outdoors to breathe in
linden and orange trees.
Time to leave.

Packed nothing, took nothing –
oh, perhaps a black trash bag over
his shoulder, trudging away down
a muddy road like a refugee –
everywhere, anywhere.

His way of saying,
Goodbye old world.
Farewell old world,
I'm off to Siam or wherever the hell
but here I am. Began life over.

But life anew, he found,
was much like life left behind,
except now ragged, unwashed,
unsure, shoes long since worn down
to remnants that spoke to the life

he'd led, continued to lead, until the end.

Our Last Meeting at 853 Riverside Drive

It could have been a park bench   It could be we sat
far apart   Could be I tried to cry but couldn't
Perhaps I felt guilty for the way he died   I could hardly
bring myself to visit him in hospital those months –
coma, you know – Could be I should have asked more
about his life before he lost his life   Could be my
children will ask about my life   Maybe not   It could be
he tried to tell me something but his words evaporated
into blue air   It could be I whispered the mourner's
kaddish as he would have wanted me to   Could be when
he said 'I'm proud of you,' that was his kaddish *for me*
It could be –

My Father Returns to Die
at 853 Riverside Drive

His was the body I saw in coma. The accident.
The body I saw in a mortician's parlor in a plain pine
coffin, dressed in white, made up to disguise the
ravages of life: rouge, reddened lips, slicked hair –
his cheek drawing heat from my hand. The body viewed
one last time before lowered into the ground, followed by
dirt, rocks, prayers and perpetual darkness.

In medical school I dissected a formaldehyded man in his
thirties – gaunt, anonymous (I named him "Chuckie")
– stripping away skin, nerve, muscle, down to bone;
nearly nothing now, like the turkey carcass left over after
Thanksgiving, tossed into the waste.

Lost in the Maze at 853 Riverside Drive

The garden door closed behind him with a snap
No latch or handle to allow escape
He faced the curve of a high, well-trimmed hedge
    should he go left
    should he go right
His skin crawled with fear and shivering
Perhaps he could inch his way
Until he came upon a bench in an alcove
    and there he sat   a child crying
    hoping to be rescued
Until it grew dark   and he fell asleep

Brothers in Exile

FOR I AM A BRICK
(What does a brick want to be? An arch. – Louis Kahn)

For I arise from clay and return to dust.
For I laid the foundation of empires: Babylon, Rome.

For I led Dorothy unto the Land of Oz.
For I harrowed Hebrews building Pithom and Raamses.

For I can will myself into an arch –
for I am of the guild of builders.

I build students' bookshelves to hold Hesse, Gibran
and prop up a gimp-legged table.

For I make a ready pendulum attached to rope,
to plumb the depth of wells.

For I break windows by anarchists' arms.
For I scrape dog shit off my master's shoes,
and hold down his poems in a stiff breeze.

For when heated I warm my master's feet in winter.

For when so commanded I will drown kittens.
For I am at times a term of endearment.

FROM OUR BALCONY, DHOUR CHOUEIR, LEBANON

a diesel-driven tiller sputters across a patch of farm

    roosters cry up the morning

someone downstairs chopping parsley for *tabbouleh*

    dump trucks grinding gears

the pushcart seller calls out *potatoes   tomatoes
aubergine   beans*

    our neighbor's cigarette cough   hawk   spit

a wedding entourage winds up from the valley
staccato honking

    bees in the lavender   tree peepers'   glissando

shotgun shooters drop birds out of the sky

    a single dog howls a cappella

last call to prayer from a far-off mosque

    cicadas grow still   whisper of wind

at night an owl whoos softly   a rabbit squeals

THE YOUNG GUIDE AT A BEIRUT MUSEUM

and I notice her dancing hands with henna
tattoos as she enlightens us to civilisations
beneath our feet, and how archaeologists

unearth human remains, and I notice her
midnight-black eyes rimmed with kohl,
how the ancients also adorned themselves

with beauty marks, and I notice in her
eagerness we ought understand our origins,
her mouth forming a perfect bow, and how

paleo-hunters brought down their quarry.

Rita, in Egypt
(With a phrase from Mahmoud Darwish)

She sits upright on a straight-backed
metal chair, by a gap where a window was,
inside an empty depot, overlooking

a rural platform. Were I close I would
inhale the laurel-soap in the hollow of her throat.
Across the way three old men in keffiyehs

and long gowns sit under a palm. A minaret.
In the distance, someone riding a donkey.
Two boys kick a rag football through the dust.

She wears a belted polka dot dress. Were I there
I would know the bead of sweat on her upper lip,
her face in three-quarters shadow, shadow

across her *honey-coloured eyes*, tendrils
of hair descending as she looks down.
Were I nearby I could bend to hear her vibrato.

She has ended a rendezvous. A clock stops.
A train hisses into the station.

Vilhelm Hammershøi: Interiors

Green-blue foliage filtered through panes of two
Lace-curtained French windows. Stock-still on the
Right, a woman, hair in a bun, a belted black dress.

Again: black skirt, white pinafore blouse, she reads
A letter. A strand of hair uncurls, her nape,
Sweet cream skin. Now she peers out the window,

Leans forward, one knee up on a chair:
Someone coming? Someone going? Or, someone
Not yet in sight. A walnut-brown fortepiano

Against the wall, her elbows at the ready.
A twist of hair strays from her bun; all sound
Suspended. She faces the ochre wall,

Her blouse ochre, the skirt brown, her bun brown,
White nape of her neck, that loose curl. Single beds
On opposite walls by the window,

Black belted floor-length dress, hands folded
In her lap, looking out at bare trees.
Night-time shadows from a porch light or

Moonlight casting dim squares, dark mullions,
Through windows to the floor. She sits in darkness
By a small end-table, staring into the corner.

Another view, a sequence through the flat –

Room, room, porch, bare sunlight far off;
A chair, cylinder stove, miniatures
On the wall. She, now, tray on hip,

Her black dress bleeding into wall and floor.

Untitled
(After Mark Rothko)

red starburst   colossal
bruise soon to be purple
black as the coming night

black as the coming night
red starburst   colossal
bruise soon to be purple

bruise soon to be purple
black as the coming night
red starburst   colossal

MEMENTO MORI

peony blossoms
hang their heads
another springtime gone

dusty evening
two grey squirrels
spiral an ancient elm

summer shiver
someone has
walked on my grave

north wind returns
susurrus of geese
loneliness

stone thrown down a well
unknown before
unseen after

HO!

DEIR EL QAMAR*

Bone-white incense
glacial aroma of absence
chants strangled in the throat

Rising earth-light
blue angelic innocence

On the dark-side
the mad the maligned
the lost the possessed

*In Arabic, Monastery of the Moon

ONE THOUSAND AND ONE NIGHTS

Go on your way and be comforted,
*   Child of the Faithful.*
He who has moulded the world in His hands
Holds it and us in His hands forever.
What He has written cannot be altered,
What He has not written, never shall be.
So go on your way and be comforted,
*   Child of the Faithful.*

Misery without dying, the toll we pay
to live, the obols we store.
What more to say?
Go on your way and be comforted.

Inside each brain, a singular universe:
Cornell boxes filled with bric-a-brac
[Ace of spades, anemones, desiccated butterflies]
By He who has moulded the world in His hands.

So little time, how dare we waste?
But waste is what we do best
just to stay alive; our lives mere toys –
He holds them and us in His hands forever.

Who is this 'He' and by what right
to give and take a plangent world
to waste then withdraw as if
What He has written cannot be altered?

It seems so. Everything we do
contingent on every instant passing.
Free will? To grind your teeth!
What He has not written, never shall be.

When someone shuts my final hours,
when my neural circuits go down,
I'll be a black mirror known to none.
So, go on your way, and be comforted,
   Child of the Faithful.

On Misreading the First Verse
of an Ancient Hebrew Hymn

And Moses asked...what are these windows
of heaven? And He said to him, these windows are:

Widows of weeping
   Widows of guns
Widows of famine
   Widows with dead sons

   Widows of cholera
Widows of doubt
   Widows of ruins
Widows without

Widows with crossbows
   Widows on thrones
Widows against the wall
   Widows of stones

   Widows of long white gloves
Widows of silk
   Widows of attar
Widows of poison milk

Widows in lifeboats
   Widows at checkpoints
Widows beneath a hunchback moon
   Widows in long black tents

and he saw – widows,
without number, without end

Brothers in Exile

I, Norbert, American physician, poet,
refugee from the genocidal regime
of Adolf Hitler.

I, Fouad, Syrian physician, poet,
refugee from the genocidal regime
of Bashar al Assad.

Brothers in exile from separate
generations, working to translate
each other –

Find here poems of painful memories
but also joy in our daily encounters.
Together,

we try build a small space for happiness. Read on.

Déjà Vu

As yesterday in Aleppo, so today in Beirut:
Syrians came as guests but now the host is leaving.
Friends have gone, one by one –
No day without a message, or phone call, or news:
I'm in Istanbul, Berlin, I'm in Montreal.
I am everywhere.

The thread of the rosary snapped; beads scattered.
Frightened, wounded, oppressed,
Chased by geography's curse, history's misery,
And this dark present.

A pattern enduring:
One builds a life piece by piece – demolished by a
barrel bomb.
Rebuilds a life – flattened by ammonium nitrate
hidden in the harbor.
Builds yet again – ravaged by tyrants, bankers,
corrupt dogs greedy for meat.

The thread frays. One glass bead falls from the
tenth floor. Nonsense to ask where it lands.

Fouad M. Fouad
Co-translated from Arabic with Norbert Hirschhorn

EXCERPTS FROM 'DIARY OF A LOSS'

Day 6
We prepare for the worst,
Then when the worst comes
We're dumbfounded, shocked
And we flounder, begin again,

Preparing for the worst.
We will know the names
Of the killers but not the killed.
Even in death, History is unjust.

Day 12
My books are also refugees. Thousands arrived today
from my library in Aleppo. Books I'd collected over
forty years, arriving at the University's warehouse in
brown and white cartons like coffins, lying there awaiting
their new home. What a long journey they passed, what
harrowing negotiations to transport them out of my
house, my clinic. (This story deserves a long talk with
fewer fevered words... someday.) The books plead for
refuge, having taken great risk to reach safety.

My books: memories, stories, notes tucked between
pages, glosses in the margins; books yet unread and
books scarred from so many readings. Secret treasures
smuggled within the trucks' chassis, trucks like that one
in Austria hiding Syrian families who suffocated. Other
books I had to abandon like a helpless father unable to
protect his children. Other books I gave away, like the
tender father who knows they will be loved. My books
are now in store rooms, stacked like bodies in a morgue,
or in hidey-holes, bastards among thousands of others.

Day 14
This morning, another old friend left Aleppo.
Whether for good or just temporarily, whether forced
or (somehow) voluntarily, I lose. Another loss, a kind of
loss like an extracted tooth, a death in small doses, which
doesn't ease the pain only making it chronic, drawn out.

Day 16
Other friends meet their exile
in their new homes: the grave.

Most hurtful are those who slip out
the back gate of friendship,
leaving me bewildered.
I reach out only to get my fingers bitten.

One after another they mutate into suitcases,
waiting rooms, or a plain text-message reading,
         Arrived safely.
What do people in jail remember?
Do they remember their birthdays?
The eldest sister lights a candle,
then another and another so
he will not get lost on his way back to her.

Fouad M. Fouad
Co-translated from Arabic with Norbert Hirschhorn

In the Beginning

YOU & I

You the helmsman & I a ship adrift
Who else to pilot me into safe haven

You the potter & I primal clay
Who else to waken my true form within

You the gardener & I a small weed
Who else shall rain mercy upon my rare flower

You the tailor & I scrap of cloth
Who else to stitch me into fine motley

You the wainwright & I a broken spoke
Who else to heal this injured wheel

You the scribe & I blank vellum
Who else shall enscroll me as psalm   as poem

I Dream of Him in Lightness and Dust

Again, last night, I'm running down a dirt trail,
the sun on my face in a yellow haze,
dust puffing up against my ankles.

In the distance, a shimmer of young spring willows
and I see him, waiting, at a fork in the road.
My breath, heart, steps quicken

but he vanishes through the thickening scrim.
When I stop to rest, he reappears, nearer,
half-turned to me –

White linen suit, black bowtie, hair dark and full.
He smiles, beckons, a cigarette between
ring and middle finger, face unravaged.

Before me now, arms outstretched.
I want to fall on his breast, panting, crying,
bury my face in his sweet-smelling neck.

Instead, we press our hands together,
my right hand between his, his between mine.
For this is the manner, for this is the custom

how the dead greet the dead.

THE *TAHARA*

He died. At home. In bed. The Old Country.

His family placed the body on a linen
sheet on the floor, feet facing the door,
covered it with a second linen. When body-
washers from the *Chevra Kadisha* arrived
they began the *Tahara*, a purification.

Bed clothes removed, chin bound up,
body rubbed down with lukewarm water,
water poured over its head, water perfumed
by attar of rose or myrtle as was performed
in ancient days. They recited from
Ezekiel:

> *I will sprinkle clean water on you,*
> *cleanse you from all your impurities.*

They testified to the beauties of the body
recounting from the Song of Songs:

> *His head is burnished gold. His eyes*
> *like doves by rivers of milk and plenty.*

Hair combed, nails cleaned, nine measures
of cold water poured on the body, dried
with fleece, enshrouded by hand-sewn linen,
pieces of pottery placed over eyes and mouth,
the body laid in a plain pine box.
The family kissed his head in reverence.
Tahara, a gift to the bereaved, done.
The body now ready for burial by sundown.

LESSONS FROM A PERFECT LIFE
(For Talia on her Bat Mitsvah)

Ask the fruit seller to recite her perfect life.
Ask the old man shining shoes, the boy
delivering throwaway news, the garbage truck rider
picking it up, the blind old woman with a metal cup.

Love anything growing crooked.
Laugh 613 times a day.
Never deprive anyone of a living.
Look into the sun and sneeze.

Sit in the woods, breathing like a Buddha –
Luck's big brown eyes will fix on you
from shadows between the trees.

    Spider spins the web.
A troublesome boy rakes it with a stick.
    Spider restores her home.
Rain punctures and bunches the strands.
    Spider reinvents her life.

Listen to your old uncle: *eppes fun gurnisht*,
making something from nothing. Ah, right, right –
Living is the perfect life, just living.

Note: '613' is the number of essential commandments
in Judaism.

To Aila Maayan

Shema! Listen! A wonderful event happening each
second of September – Aila, to celebrate your
birth-days and your parents' anniversaries on that
same day, may they come for a blessing to us all.

Shema! Listen! Your gifted name, Oak, means being
steadfast, solid, strong – in Arabic *sumud*, in Hebrew
khazak, in Yiddish *fest*.

Your other gifted name, *Wellspring*, means may you
be nurtured by the waters of love, a beloved
daughter, granddaughter.

May you nurture in turn all those who come after
in the unbroken chain of *Am Yisroel* and humanity.

Even if, when you read this, I am long gone,
know your ancestors, where you have come from.

With love and hope,

Great-uncle Norbert

Noah on the Mississippi
(Sing to the Lord a new song – Psalm 96)

Birds too can hardly wait for warmer weather:
at earliest ice-out down by the storm-drain,
some mallards have reappeared.

How clever – where had they been?
How did they know?
My elderly neighbor claims they winter
on a man-warmed pond near the Mayo.

Had they been sending out daily –
like Noah's dove – a solitary duck
to reconnoiter the land? No, he says,
a crow went down to bring 'em in.

***

Cruelest day this winter, wind-chill
forty-eight below: our cardinal pair,
too weak to fly from fir to feeder,
disappeared, their bodies gone to ground.

But now all species reemerge: nuthatch,
junco, purple finch, and yes, cardinals,
newly volent princes of the high perch,

come to reanimate my world,
in celebration, two by two.

IN THE BEGINNING

was a certain bird, and the bird had an inaudible chirp,
and God saw it was good. But the bird pleaded for
identity, a sound other birds would hear, then respect.
All songs had been given out, none left, but
God took pity on this one last, tiny thing, and made its
wings beat so fast they hummed.

LETTER TO MY PARENTS LONG GONE
FROM 853 RIVERSIDE DRIVE

I think of you often,
especially on your birthdays
(July 19, November 29),
each of you divine,
your spirits nesting inside me.

You gave me life. Full stop.

What you endured to see me through:
abandoning your parents to the Shoah,
uprooted, flight, turmoil in America.

And I, know-it-all, hardly knew
what you went through – I fled,
abandoned you, even as
you stayed faithful to me.

My most sorrowful apologies,

    Your firstborn son

ACKNOWLEDGEMENTS

Sailing with the Pleiades – In the chapbook by that name, published by *Main Street Rag*

Anatomy Lesson: The Philtrum – *Rusted Radishes*

Virginia Creeper – *The Ekphrastic Review* (Based on a painting by Edward Bourne-Jones, first of four from The Briar Rose Series.)

Visitation; The Call; One Thousand and One Nights – *London Grip*

Against Solitude – *Evening Street Press & Review*

The Young Guide at a Beirut Museum; On Misreading the First Verse of an Ancient Hebrew Hymn – *Poetry Salzburg*

One Thousand and One Nights – A *glose from The Arabian Nights. An Anthology* – edited by Wen-Chin Ouyang. New York: Everyman's Library, Alfred A. Knopf, 2014.

On Misreading… With Marilyn Hacker, alternating verses; from 'The Poetry of Kabbalah', translation from the Hebrew by Peter Cole. Yale University (New Haven) 2012.

Rita, In Egypt – After Anouar Braham CD (ECM 2075), 'The Astounding Eyes of Rita,' cover photograph by Fouad ElKhoury.

Vilhelm Hammershøi: Interiors – Based on the exhibition at the British Royal Academy of Arts, 'Vilhelm Hammershøi: The Poetry of Silence,' September 2008
Poem short-listed out of 8200 entries in Bridport Prize competition (UK), 2011.

Excerpts from 'Diary of a Loss' – *New England Review*

Déjà Vu – *Michigan Quarterly Review*

Noah on the Mississippi – *La Presa*

In the Beginning – Abandoned Mine, and, a finalist in Atticus Book Store (UK) 'One Minute Monologue' competition, 2022.

The *Tahara – Chevra Kadisha,* literally 'holy society', is a group of Jewish men and women to assure the ritual of burial.

To Aila Maayan is dedicated to Talia's newborn daughter.

Poems co-translated with Fouad M. Fouad
follow on our collaboration in a bilingual collection,
Once Upon a Time in Aleppo, Hippocrates Press, London, 2020.

With gratitude to my first (and best) readers: Cynthia Myntti, Jacqueline Saphra; and to Anne-Marie Fyfe whose on-line courses prompted a number of the poems. And to my London poetry-mates who welcome me regularly via Zoom during the pandemic. And to my publisher, Holland Park Press and Bernadette Jansen op de Haar who 'publishes authors, not books'.

The Author

Norbert Hirschhorn is a public health physician, commended in 1993 by President Bill Clinton as an American Health Hero and proud to follow in the tradition of physician-poets.

He is the 2023 recipient of the Pupin Medal, conferred by Columbia University in the City of New York in recognition of his longstanding service to the nation in science.

Hirschhorn's poems have been published in over three dozen journals, and six full collections. His work has won a number of prizes in the US and UK.

Norbert Hirschhorn has published six collections:

A Cracked River, Slow Dancer Poetry, 1999
Mourning in the Presence of a Corpse, Dar al-Jadeed, 2008
Monastery of the Moon Dar al-Jadeed, 2012
To Sing Away the Darkest Days – Poems Re-imagined from Yiddish Folk Songs, Holland Park Press, 2013
Stone. Bread. Salt., Holland Park Press, 2018
Once Upon a Time in Aleppo, a bilingual Arabic-English co-translation with Syrian physician-poet Fouad M. Fouad, The Hippocrates Press, 2020

More information is available from his website, www.bertzpoet.com.

His memoir, *To Heal the World: My Life in Medicine, Poetry, and Public Health* is available as an ebook from Sloan Publishing (Cornwall on Hudson, NY), 2022, https://sloanpublishing.com, and from www.bertzpoet.com.

Holland Park Press, founded in 2009, is a privately-owned independent company publishing literary fiction: novels, novellas, short stories; and poetry. The company is run by brother and sister team Arnold and Bernadette Jansen op de Haar, who publish an author not just a book. Holland Park Press specialises in finding new literary talent by accepting unsolicited manuscripts from authors all year round and by running competitions. It has been successful in giving older authors a chance to make their debut and in raising the profile of Dutch authors in translation.

To

Learn more about Norbert Hirschhorn
Discover other interesting books
Read our blogs and news items
Find out how to submit your manuscript
Take part in one of our competitions

Visit www.hollandparkpress.co.uk

Bookshop: http://www.hollandparkpress.co.uk/books.php

Holland Park Press in the social media:

https://www.twitter.com/HollandParkPres
https://www.facebook.com/HollandParkPress
https://www.linkedin.com/company/holland-park-press
https://www.youtube.com/user/HollandParkPress
https://www.instagram.com/hollandparkpress/